THINGS ARE COMPLETELY SIMPLE

Illuminations: A Series on American Poetics

Series Editor: Jon Thompson

Illuminations focuses on the poetics and poetic practices of the contemporary moment in the USA. The series is particularly keen to promote a set of reflective works that include, but go beyond, traditional academic prose, so we take Walter Benjamin's rich, poetic essays published under the title of *Illuminations* as an example of the kind of approach we most value. Collectively, the titles published in this series aim to engage various audiences in a dialogue that will reimagine the field of contemporary American poetics. For more about the series, please visit its website at parlorpress.com/illuminations.

Books in the Series

Things Are Completely Simple: Poetry and Translation by Brian Henry
The Poet's Tomb: The Material Soul of Poetry by Martin Corless-Smith
Vestiges: Notes, Responses, and Essays 1988–2018 by Eric Pankey
Sudden Eden by Donald Revell
Prose Poetry and the City by Donna Stonecipher

THINGS ARE COMPLETELY SIMPLE

POETRY AND TRANSLATION

Brian Henry

Parlor Press
Anderson, South Carolina
www.parlorpress.com

Parlor Press LLC, Anderson, South Carolina, USA

Printed in the United States of America on acid-free paper.
S A N: 2 5 4 - 8 8 7 9

Library of Congress Cataloging-in-Publication Data on File

Names: Henry, Brian, 1972- author.
Title: Things are completely simple : poetry and translation / Brian Henry.
Description: Anderson, South Carolina : Parlor Press, 2022. | Series: Illuminations: a series on American poetics | Includes bibliographical references. | Summary: "Things Are Completely Simple examines poetry and translation from an accomplished poet-translator's perspective. The book's polyphonic structure puts different translators, writers, and theorists in conversation with each other"-- Provided by publisher.
Identifiers: LCCN 2021051106 (print) | LCCN 2021051107 (ebook) | ISBN 9781643172903 (paperback) | ISBN 9781643172910 (pdf) | ISBN 9781643172927 (epub)
Subjects: LCSH: Poetry--Translating.
Classification: LCC PN1059.T7 H46 2022 (print) | LCC PN1059.T7 (ebook) | DDC 418/.041--dc23/eng/20211206
LC record available at https://lccn.loc.gov/2021051106
LC ebook record available at https://lccn.loc.gov/2021051107

2 3 4 5

Illuminations: A Series on American Poetics
Series Editor: Jon Thompson

Cover image by Hostaphoto on Unsplash.
Interior and cover design: David Blakesley

Parlor Press, LLC is an independent publisher of scholarly and trade titles in print and multimedia formats. This book is available in paper and eBook formats from Parlor Press on the World Wide Web at http://www.parlorpress.com or through online and brick-and-mortar bookstores. For submission information or to find out about Parlor Press publications, write to Parlor Press, 3015 Brackenberry Drive, Anderson, South Carolina, 29621, or email editor@parlorpress.com.

Contents

i.m. Tomaž Šalamun

Preface

This book adopts an unconventional, nonlinear format, combining others' and my reflections on translation as both a discipline and a critical/creative act, my thoughts on the translation process, and excerpts from correspondence with poets whose work I've translated. My ideas about translation are advanced both in individual passages and via juxtaposition; others' ideas about translation overlap and conflict with each other and with my own. Partly because the art of translation is a collaboration, I purposely avoid presenting a single voice or perspective here. My aim is not to convince readers that my methods of translation should prevail over other methods. I welcome multiple approaches and attitudes toward translation, as well as multiple translations of individual poems. I care most about what translation means for poetry. Poetry is an art of possibility, and translation expands the range of what's possible.

Acknowledgments

Parts of this book first appeared on the *Best American Poetry* site and in *Blackbird*, *Denver Quarterly*, *Poetry*, *Transom*, and *The Volta*. Many thanks to the editors.

Things Are Completely Simple

“[T]he reflection on translation has become an internal necessity of translation itself . . .” —Antoine Berman, *The Experience of the Foreign* (1)

“Contemporary literary translation is a minefield. Some of the issues are clear enough—whether, for example, one attempts to bring the poem to the reader by smoothing out its eccentricities and aiming for the most beautiful (and *familiar*) poem in the target language, or attempts instead to bring the reader to the poem by reproducing as best one can its strangeness and particular character—but the manner in which, in any given locus, one resolves or juggles them is not.” —David Brooks, “Srečko Kosovel: Life and Poetry” (11–12)

*

"A translated text . . . is judged acceptable by most publishers, reviewers, and readers when it reads fluently, when the absence of any linguistic or stylistic peculiarities makes it seem transparent, giving the appearance that it reflects the foreign writer's personality or intention or the essential meaning of the foreign text—the appearance, in other words, that the translation is not in fact a translation, but the 'original.'" —Lawrence Venuti, *The Translator's Invisibility* (1)

"[T]he difference between a translation and the original is not a difference in the texts themselves. I suppose if we did not know which was the original and which was the translation, we could judge them fairly. But, unhappily, we cannot do this. And so the translator's work is always supposed to be inferior—or, what is worse, is *felt* to be inferior—even though, verbally, the rendering may be as good as the text." —Jorge Luis Borges, "Word-Music and Translation" (65)

"[T]ranslation is the prosthetic that calls attention to its own un-naturalness . . ." —Joyelle McSweeney and Johannes Göransson, "Manifesto of the Disabled Text"

*

Willingly or no, translators work with Arthur Schopenhauer's dictum—"Poems cannot be translated, they can only be transposed" (33)—in the background. John Felstiner's qualification seems somewhat more reassuring: "Let us admit that to really translate a poem is impossible—impossible yet fascinating . . ." (27). In the discourse on translation, especially poetry translation, translation has become the art of can't.

Referring to the literature on translation from the past 200+ years, Daniel Tiffany remarks upon "the absurdity (and potency) of a discourse that starts from the premise of its own non-existence . . .": "given the eerie uniformity of historical opinion regarding the impossibility of translation, it is hard not to detect a trace of fanaticism, an overture to what exceeds language and reasoning—a demonology, as though in defending the idea of untranslatability one sought to maintain an *impossible* position" (176–77).

Tiffany identifies "untranslatability" as the "distinguishing feature of poetic texts." Yet, as he reminds us by quoting Novalis, "To translate is to write poetry as much as creating one's own works" (180).

The "Impossible Effigies" chapter in Tiffany's *Radio Corpse* examines the fetishistic, haunted, "phantasmatic," crypt-ic, zombie-esque, channeling, and even "abusive" aspects of translating the dead. "There is a terrible risk, of course, in feeding the dead from the store of one's own vitality" (191). He also points out that "Death, it would seem, is all but inescapable in translation; in its wake, we are apt to be set upon by a ghost, or to discover a corpse (of the original, of the translator's text and her language, of meaning, and so on). . . . [B]y evoking death, translation discourse . . . evokes the impossible, the unknowable, the ineffable" (186).

*

The title of American poet Christian Hawkey's book *Ventrakl* combines "ventricle" and the surname of German poet Georg Trakl, while also gesturing toward "ventriloquy," an apt title for a sustained attempt to reach the dead poet. Throughout *Ventrakl*, Hawkey summons Trakl, "interviews" him, and works "with" him while engaging with Trakl's poems, photographs, and biography. Hawkey's attempt at friendship necessarily remains a futile one, however hard he tries to bring Trakl into the room. Identified as "a collaboration," *Ventrakl* cannot be a true collaboration between (near-)equals, but is one in which the only active and willing participant (the living poet) manipulates various aspects of the work and life of the passive participant (the dead poet). Trakl's solitary nature, his addictions, his difficult family life, and his attraction to (and ultimate success at) suicide make him an unlikely collaborator—certainly less likely than Jack Spicer's Lorca, the most salient precursor to Hawkey's Trakl. Because Hawkey approaches Trakl less as a professional translator seeking a source than as a poet seeking a kindred spirit, this lack of actual connection becomes both a point of regret and a driving force for Hawkey. *Ventrakl* emerges as a complex seance as well as a significant work of "transwriting."

Ventrakl's first 'chapter,' "Neither of Us Is Powerless," offers a hopeful assertion but also, finally, an impossible one. The impossibility of Hawkey's aim here is a large part of what makes *Ventrakl* so fascinating and troubling—the inevitable futility of, yet Hawkey's persistence in, calling to Trakl in these pages. The title appears at the end of Hawkey's meditation on a photograph of Trakl:

> You seem and do not seem to be holding a cigarette, the chewed end of a cigar, a shell. It seems to me a small camera pointed at the one taking the photograph, the one for whom you pretend not to be posing.

> I see you, you seem to say. Neither of us is powerless. (21)

But Trakl's "power" is illusory, projected by Hawkey even if felt by him. Trakl is not, cannot be, holding a small camera. He cannot be turning a lens back onto the photographer. Hawkey's gesture here, his desire to animate Trakl, transfer authority to Trakl, or at least share authority with him, is bound to fail, yet does so poignantly.

"Neither of Us Is Powerless" opens with a direct address to Trakl in that photograph: "You are, clearly, on a beach" (17). That word *clearly*, which here means something like "evidently" or "obviously" (since it's obvious that Trakl is standing on a beach), acquires additional resonance because in *Ventrakl* so little is actually clear. By beginning with an irrefutable statement, Hawkey seems to be preparing himself, and us, for the numerous irresolvabilities that follow. It's as if Hawkey needs to begin on firm ground before moving into the murk.

In his musings on the beach scene, Hawkey connects what he sees behind Trakl—"the mother and two children in the background . . . standing (it seems) on the surface of the mineral-heavy water; the mother lowers a string into the depths, the boy tilts toward her, the girl stands one step back from the hole"—to Trakl's seemingly benign but suddenly fraught posture in the photograph: "you, leaning forward as if running—or falling—into the hole, the chloroform hole, the cigarette hole, the opium hole, the morphine hole, the veronal hole, the cocaine hole, the mouth hole, the nose hole, the vein hole, the food hole, the language hole, breathing hole, word hole." "Here," Hawkey writes, "a history of holes and what we put inside them, lose inside them" (19). *Ventrakl*, then, is a book of holes—holes in biography, holes in the poems' transference from one language to another, holes in the poems themselves (as when Hawkey ostensibly prepares a translation with a shotgun).

This intense seeing with the photographs also transfers to Hawkey's practice of reading. Homophonic and homographic translations form a major current of *Ventrakl*, as a living American poet makes poems by Englishing a dead German poet's work, recalling the "Impossible Effigies" chapter in Tiffany's *Radio Corpse*. Hawkey himself remarks on "the singular performances of decay and decomposition" in *Ventrakl*, and muses, "perhaps when I leave this room I should see myself as a corpse, a zombie, a limb thudding onto the floor . . ." (92). Hawkey's strategy here also nods to George Steiner's notion of translation as "interanimation," which is "a process of totally attentive interpenetration" that leads to "the establishment of mutual identity through conjunction" (476).

Within the context of *Ventrakl*, some of Hawkey's homophonic translations of Trakl seem curious if not questionable. They present the reader with a unique challenge, since Hawkey employs different translation techniques but never specifically identifies them. The reader, then, does not know how to read many of the poems in relation to the originals. This is, of course, intentional, and Hawkey clearly wants the reader to feel a certain level of discomfort, or at least uncertainty. At one point, Hawkey claims that he wanted "to trouble [Walter] Benjamin's distinctions between poet and translator" (7), and elsewhere he asks "Who is writing then?" (37). In a way, he is illuminating the slippage of translation itself, challenging the conventions of what a poem, a translation, and a collaboration should be, working to stretch—not to satisfy—the reader's expectations. Just as the reader of *Ventrakl* cannot tell how faithfully rendered a particular translation is, how much is Hawkey and how much is Trakl, any poem translated from one language into another, however faithfully, presents a similar problem: the translator's involvement, or encroachment. At times, Hawkey uses phrases that *reflect upon* rather than *emanate from* Trakl's poems: "Only sounds, dissected, profit you" (31). Such moments offer fleeting interpretations dependent on Hawkey's time and culture, Trakl's time, and Hawkey's understanding of Trakl's poetry and knowledge of Trakl's life. Sometimes, though, Hawkey's creative translations unnecessarily obscure or outshine the original.

Consider "Dust Rounds," a homophonic version of Trakl's "Das Grauen," or "The Horror," which in the original reads:

Das Grauen

Ich sah mich durch verlass'ne Zimmer gehn.
Die Sterne tanzten irr auf blauem Grunde,
Und auf den Feldern heulten laut die Hunde,
Und in den Wipfeln wühlte wild der föhn.

Doch plötzlich: Stille! Dumpfe Fieberglut
Läßt giftige Blumen blühn aus meinem Munde,
Aus dem Geäst fällt wie aus einer Wunde
Blaß schimmernd Tau, und fällt, und fällt wie Blut.

Aus eines Spiegels trügerischer Leere
Hebt langsam sich, und wie ins Ungefähre
Aus Graun und Finsternis ein Antlitz: Kain!

Sehr leise rauscht die samtene Portiere,
Durchs Fenster schaut der Mond gleichwie ins Leere,
Da bin mit meinem Mörder ich allein.

Here is my conventional translation of the poem:

The Horror

I watched myself walk through abandoned rooms.
Stars were dancing madly on the blue ground,
And in the fields dogs howled loud,
And in the treetops the wind moved wild.

But suddenly: silence! A dull feverglow
Makes poisonous flowers bloom from my mouth,
Pale shimmering dew falls from the branches
As from a wound, and falls, and falls like blood.

From a mirror's deceptive emptiness
A face rises slow and vague
From the horror and darkness: Cain!

So quiet the velvet curtain's rustling,
The moon gazes through the window as into emptiness,
I am alone there with my murderer.

Hawkey transmutes Trakl's German into

Dust Rounds

I saw dust mites lurch through deserted rooms.
I saw a tungsten-blue blossom on her sternum.

A plot licks stillness. Dumbness fevers
The last albumen effigies of a miniature world.

Only geese with kindness shimmer
And, once blasted, fall in red blurts.

Down a loneliness-stick inner spangles
Issue tears, and we in unguent failure

Are drawn to this spinsterish ant-light.
Note, for example, the red eyes of sumptuous porters.

The orphans shouting at fences. How they glisten,
At night, with the dimwit mien of an alien order. (32)

Clearly, the meaning of the original has been cast aside. That's what homophonic translation does. Homophonic translations (and imitations) generally attempt to create an independent poem in the target language (in this case, English), with the source text serving more as a springboard than as an actual source.

Hawkey's vision of dust mites lurching through abandoned rooms is intentionally absurd, whereas Trakl's vision is meant to be unsettling. For many contemporary readers, Hawkey's "Dust Rounds" is probably more compelling than Trakl's "The Horror." Hawkey's poem is witty, unpredictable, au courant—it applies a patina of archaism in reverse. The poem includes geese, "sumptuous porters," orphans, and spangles; and its ending—"How they glisten, / At night, with the dimwit mien of an alien order"—is stunning in its beautiful strangeness. But Hawkey has overshadowed Trakl, recalling Rosmarie Waldrop's claim, "I have long held that translating involves envy, usurpation, and pleasure in destruction" (145), but without Waldrop's later attempt to "make reparation" (138). In a way, *Ventrakl* itself can be seen as an attempt to make reparation for the 19 homophonic translations that use Trakl's poems as a stepping stool, making Trakl the lesser partner in this collaboration, which can seem more appropriation than collaboration. Aesthetically, some of Hawkey's homophonic translations substitute a veneer of strangeness for real strangeness; rather than foreignize, they domesticate; rather than unsettle, they seem quite comfortable within the contemporary American poetic idiom.

The homophonic translations also can seem ethnocentric, as Trakl's poems are "heard" by a U.S. English-language poet preoccupied with the Iraq War. Of course, Trakl's own experience with World War I affects not only his poetry but also any subsequent reading of his poetry. Where Trakl's war poems tend to be haunting, Hawkey's lean toward the slapstick, as in "A duck fart woke the golden Karen" (63), "Ashcroft with his round, condom-colored eyes" (117), "Nuns wearing Diesel jeans" (84), and "Wild dorks hide in the bushes of Holland" (51). Elsewhere we have Visa, New Balance, Nissan, Starbucks, "Ford-tough" (80), Ewoks, and Aussies. In this kind of "collaboration," Hawkey inevitably will bring his own cultural noise and detritus into the mix. What Hawkey hears and finds depends on the time and place of his listening and looking.

As Venuti notes in *The Translator's Invisibility*, "The ethnocentric violence of translation is inevitable: in the translation process, foreign languages, texts, and cultures always undergo some degree and form of exclusion, reduction, and inscription that reflect the cultural situation in the translating language" (267). The translator's goal, then, should be to minimize or mitigate this violence, not to exacerbate it, even if the translator's own needs (e.g., wanting to respond to the Iraq war) call for it. When viewed in a less generous light, Hawkey's homophonic translations can be seen as the offal of what Serge Gavronsky describes as the "aggressive translator." This kind of translator "seizes possession of the 'original' . . . and truly feeds upon the words" before he then "enunciates them in his own tongue." In the end, "the original is mutilated beyond recognition" (60). In seeking the familiar (domestic) within the strange (foreign), homophonic translation enacts a kind of narcissism, where the reader/perceiver recognizes self in the presence of something other.

However, as André Lefevere notes in an essay on Bertolt Brecht, "A writer's work gains exposure and achieves influence mainly through 'misunderstandings and misconceptions,' or, to use a more neutral term, refractions" (204). Another way to consider Hawkey's mistranslations, then, would be as a roundabout attempt to make Trakl more visible through refraction. Rather than being read through World War I, Trakl's work, thanks to Hawkey, can be read against the war in Iraq, albeit in a sometimes disconcerting way. Hawkey himself seems to back away from the translation process when he writes, "not a poem translated from another but a poem woven around another, from another" (45): "transwriting" rather than translating.

The homophonic translations, however numerous and prevalent, are in the end not what mark *Ventrakl* as an important book. *Ventrakl*'s achievement consists in its blend of these creative translations with color-coded centos, biographical prose, lyric prose, numbered lists (e.g., "Notes Toward the Translation of Facial Expressions"), discussions of process, italicized prose passages recounting Trakl's and Hawkey's "visits," "interviews" with Trakl, and prose on photographs.

Hawkey's eight "interviews" with Trakl throughout the book are, necessarily, interviews with Hawkey handling both Q and A; they're closer to poems, such as Tomaž Šalamun's "Jonah," or flashes of unconventional drama. They average five questions and responses each, and thus do not occupy much space, but they represent Hawkey's most transparent attempt to call forth Trakl. Hawkey's prose meditations on various photographs of Trakl become meditations on absence, and as such are particularly moving, as much for what they reveal of Trakl as for what they show of Hawkey as observer, obsessive, other.

Rainer Maria Rilke described the "rising and fading tones" in Trakl's poetry as "irretrievably singular," and figures that "even one who stands nearby" to Trakl would see things "as though pressed, an exile, against a pane of glass." Hawkey seeks to become a companion but remains an outsider, on the other side of the glass, for "Trakl's life passes as in mirror-images and fills its entire space, which cannot be entered, like the space in a mirror" (Trakl 19–20). This might explain why *Ventrakl* ends not with an interview or a consideration of a photograph or a homophonic translation, but with a conventional translation of Trakl's most famous poem "Grodek"—the only translation of this kind in the book. Hawkey has given up trying to connect with Trakl and has stepped back, translator rather than unsuccessful collaborator. Hawkey has realized that "perhaps ['Grodek'] demands a specific category of translation: a faithful one" (78), agreeing to meet Trakl on Trakl's terms, on his terrain.

*

> "If the foreign is unambiguously incomprehensible, unknowable, and unfamiliar, it is impossible to talk about translation, because translation simply cannot be done. If, on the other hand, the foreign is comprehensible, knowable, and familiar, it is unnecessary to call for translation. Thus the status of the foreign in translation must always be ambiguous. It is alien, but it is already in transition to something familiar. The foreign is simultaneously incomprehensible and comprehensible, unknowable and knowable, and unfamiliar and familiar."
> —Naoki Sakai, "Translation and the Figure of Border" (32)

Fewer than three percent of the books published in the United States each year have been translated from other languages.

Most readers approach translations with two seemingly contradictory attitudes: romanticization and skepticism. On the one hand, the translation has the aura of the exotic, like a tropical vacation for the mind or, for the more sensitive reader, a window onto another world (albeit a window safely distant). On the other hand, the translation seems suspect, especially if not in flawless and fluid English, with the translation bound to emerge a lesser, perhaps even degraded, version of the original.

Translation has often been described as an act of interpretation. Like criticism, translation requires a primary text, a source. But unlike criticism, the translation becomes a parallel primary text—an unequal, almost automatically inferior one, even if the translation can reach more readers than the original, even if the translation "reads better" in the target language than the original reads in the source language.

The translator always has something to prove. According to conventional wisdom and most critics, any hiccups, clunkers, or head-scratchers must be the fault of the translator. Any deviation from normative syntax must be the result of a rush job, failure to revise, mental lapse, or basic deficiency in the translator, not intentional awkwardness or discordance on the part of the author.

In *After Babel*, George Steiner describes the role of the translator as being "exercised in a radical tension between impulses to facsimile and impulses to appropriate" (235). In practice, this tension is stretched between two poles: literal word-for-word transcription and complete reinterpretation or imitation. Both sides can justify their methods, as can everyone working in between.

> "The term 'literal translation' is tautological since anything but that is not truly a translation but an imitation, an adaptation or a parody." —Vladimir Nabokov, "Problems of Translation" (134)

> "Every culture resists translation, even if it has an essential need for it. The very aim of translation—to open up in writing a certain relation with the Other, to fertilize what is one's Own through the mediation of what is Foreign—is diametrically opposed to the ethnocentric structure of every culture, that species of narcissism by which every society wants to be a pure and unadulterated Whole. There is a tinge of the violence of cross-breeding in translation." —Antoine Berman, *The Experience of the Foreign* (4)

Translation "generates an excess of poets and lineages, . . . of interpretations and languages. Perhaps most importantly, it creates an excess in the text itself: there is not just one version, there are endless versions. . . . the poem is not the exact words of the 'original.'" —Johannes Göransson, "The Immigrant Is Transposition Kitsch"

"As I read the original work, I admire it. I am overwhelmed. I would like to have written it. Clearly, I am envious—envious enough to make it mine at all cost, at the cost of destroying it. Worse, I take pleasure in destroying the work exactly because it means making it mine. And I assuage what guilt I might feel by promising that I will make reparation, that I will labor to restore the destroyed beauty in my language—also, of course, by the knowledge that I do not actually touch the original within its own language." —Rosmarie Waldrop, "The Joy of the Demiurge" (138)

*

"Translating is reading, reading of the best, the most essential, kind." —William Gass, *Reading Rilke* (50)

"[T]ranslation is the most intimate act of reading." —Gayatri C. Spivak, "The Politics of Translation" (183)

"To translate is to 'metaphor,' to 'carry across.' Translations are transpositions, reenactments, interpretations." —A.K. Ramanujan, "On Translating a Tamil Poem" (61–62)

"Either the translator leaves the author in peace as much as possible and moves the reader toward him; or he leaves the reader in peace as much as possible and moves the writer toward him." —Friedrich Schleiermacher, "On the Different Methods of Translating" (49)

"In its encounter with the original, translation requires apprehension—apprehension in the sense of 'understanding' but also in the sense of 'fear.'" —Lyn Hejinian, *The Language of Inquiry* (305)

"The appropriative 'rapture' of the translator—the word has in it, of course, the root and meaning of violent transport—leaves the original with a dialectically enigmatic residue. Unquestionably there is a dimension of loss, of breakage . . . But the residue is also, and decisively, positive. The work translated is enhanced." —George Steiner, *After Babel* (316)

"[T]ranslation concerns everything belonging to the domain of metamorphosis, transformation, imitation, recreation, copy, echo, etc." —Antoine Berman, *The Experience of the Foreign* (85)

"If we say of the simulacrum that it is a copy of a copy, an infinitely degraded icon, an infinitely loose resemblance, we then miss the essential, that is, the difference in nature between simulacrum and copy . . . The copy is an image endowed with resemblance, the simulacrum is an image without resemblance. The catechism . . . has familiarized us with this notion. God made man in his image and resemblance. Through sin, however, man lost the resemblance while maintaining the image. We have become simulacra. We have forsaken moral existence in order to enter into aesthetic existence." —Gilles Deleuze, *The Logic of Sense* (257)

"[T]he dominance of individualistic assumptions makes translation itself a minor genre of writing in English, marginal in relation to writing that not only implements the major aesthetic of transparency, but bears the authorial imprimatur." —Lawrence Venuti, *The Translator's Invisibility* (251)

*

Translators who work with dead authors from a distant past face an especially challenging task. Idioms within the source language have evolved, local and international cultures have changed (or even vanished), and the author's intentions must be discovered or intuited. Such diachronic and synchronic translation requires linguistic dexterity, historical and cultural knowledge, and devoted scholarship, which are daunting but not necessarily prohibitive obstacles. For me, the main barrier is not being able to ask the author questions, to make sure a specific word or phrase is accomplishing what it needs to. I generally feel like I can complete 95% of a translation by myself, but I sometimes need the author's input on that remaining 5%—that last little bit that I cannot quite resolve to my total satisfaction. I have translated a handful of poems by dead poets, and the results never seem entirely finished. I want to be able to communicate with whomever I'm translating—for practical reasons, but also because, for me, the best way to overcome the "impossibility" of translation is to approach it as an act of friendship, a *living* act. Every translation I do makes its way to the original author, which is an essential part of the process.

This is the crucial difference between writing poems and translating poems. Many of my own poems remain with me for weeks, months, even years before venturing out; some are never seen by anyone else. My poems are guaranteed only one reader. But my translations of living poets are guaranteed two readers, and there is always an exchange in and around the text being translated.

In "Breaking the Translation Curtain: The Homophonic Sublime," Charles Bernstein notes that "Translation is always a form of collaboration" (10). In my own translation work, I have taken Bernstein's claim literally. As I wrote in the introduction to Aleš Debeljak's *Smugglers*, I view translation as "a gesture of friendship through the word, an outcome and expression of camaraderie" (11). This recalls Paul Celan's notion that there is little difference between a poem and a handshake as well as Nazim Hikmet's description of reading poetry in translation as "a kiss through a veil." Translation as an act of friendship also might explain why I have approached translating Tomaž Šalamun, Aleš Šteger, and Debeljak somewhat differently, rather than applying my personal practice and/or theory of translation to the poets' work. If my approach chafes the author, I modify it or, if I feel strongly about it, I make my case. As a friendship does not mean imposing oneself on another, translation does not mean imposing oneself on a text. For me, translation, in this dynamic, is a shared activity that happens to require a lot of solitude.

"The essence of translation is to be an opening, a dialogue, a cross-breeding, a decentering. Translation is 'a putting in touch with,' or it is *nothing*." —Antoine Berman, *The Experience of the Foreign* (4)

*

The poets I have translated are themselves occasional translators of poetry. In many cases, their choices of poets to translate intersect with my own poetics and in turn give me insight into their poems. Debeljak translated a volume of selected poems by John Ashbery, which helped me think through Debeljak's use of digressions in his poems, just as knowing about Debeljak's affinity for poets like Celan, Trakl, and Rilke helped me understand the historical, political, and lyrical aspects of his work. Šteger has translated Spanish- and German-language writers such as Pablo Neruda, Ingeborg Bachmann, César Vallejo, and Walter Benjamin, showing as much range in the choices of what he translates as he does in his own writing. Knowing how deeply he has engaged with their work allows me to catch allusions, techniques, and concerns that I might otherwise miss.

Šalamun translated volumes of selected poems by Charles Simic and James Tate into Slovenian, and Simic was one of Šalamun's earliest English translators. The connections between Šalamun and Simic go beyond poetry, of course: they were born three years apart in the same country (Yugoslavia), lived through World War II as young children and grew up in its aftermath, and were raised speaking multiple languages. Both were deeply influenced by radical European poetry and by the rich linguistic and cultural dimensions of Yugoslavia. The dark and absurd humor in both Simic's and Tate's poetry also exists in Šalamun's, but Šalamun's work—perhaps because there is so much more of it—also exhibits more tonal and formal range. Šalamun followed American poetry as closely as he followed Slovenian poetry, including emerging poets. Knowing about his evolving affinities for various American poets sometimes informs my translations, particularly when I think of the poets he was most interested in at the time he wrote specific poems.

Many of Šalamun's own poems also already contain a certain amount of self-translation. Although written in Slovenian, they include words and phrases in Croatian, English, French, German, Italian, and Spanish. While deeply involved and invested in the Slovenian language, his poems demonstrate a polyglot's openness to other languages as non-Slovenian phrases come to mind during composition. This allows Šalamun to incorporate sounds, tones, juxtapositions, and utterances not available in his native language.

*

Bodies, too, are translated. We carry ourselves across space and time. Poetry is tied to the body—the breath, the heartbeat, flesh, movement—so knowledge of how a poet moves through the world can provide information about their work, whether one is reading it for pleasure or for the purposes of translation.

When I translate poems by Šalamun, Debeljak, or Šteger, I always picture them in my mind as I work toward finding a rhythm and music for the poem in English. I recall how they walk—in New York, in Ljubljana, in an airport, in the countryside or a college town—how they eat and drink and smoke, how they drive, how they present themselves when giving a reading, how they greet friends, how they dance and argue and cajole. All of these negotiations with the world influence their poems, and I keep them in mind so I am not just working with words on a page.

"When you translate a writer's work, where is the writer? Obviously he is not there, in the place where you walk around or lie or sit, wringing your hands, translating what he wrote, murmuring the words. . . . Yet, afterwards, *he has been there*. . . . He has been where you translated him. The work, and the passion of translating, place him there *afterwards*. Not physically, not altogether fantastically either, but in a sense that we invoke . . . when we say that rays of feeling surround, penetrate, and situate a particular object. This work of translation, as a kind of sensitive passion, unfolds through two successive moments of *Einfühlung*. First, obviously, you enter into a relationship with the writer as a presence which pervades the original text—a presence, that is, rather than a personality. Second, from that relationship, as your translation comes into the open, the writer as a presence is released into the place in which you worked . . . The bond which guarantees that presence in the place is now your translation, the text you have conducted out of the original." —Christopher Middleton, "Translation as a Species of Mime" (23–24)

*

The translator becomes the writer's amaneunsis—the ghost writer who just might get their name on the title page. Like the ghost writer, the translator usually receives no royalties or control over the work after it has been published. The translation becomes a job, a work for hire, not intellectual property.

> "[T]he more precisely the translation adheres to the turns and figures of the original, the more foreign it will seem to its reader." —Friedrich Schleiermacher, "On the Different Methods of Translating" (53)

> "The more fluent the translation, the more invisible the translator . . ." —Lawrence Venuti, *The Translator's Invisibility* (1)

*

According to Tiffany, Ezra Pound's "translations are not quite texts, or objects, or phantoms, but are amalgams of all three: verbal effigies of powerful literary figures from the past whom he alternately reveres and abuses according to the present needs of his own poetic project" (219).

> "Translation is a suicidal art. It is translation which generates and sustains the metaphysics of the untranslatable and the prestige of the 'original' creative writing at its own expense." —Clive Scott, *Translating Baudelaire* (69)

*

Šalamun largely agreed with Vladimir Nabokov, for whom the only worthwhile translation is an entirely literal one. Šalamun, however, was not interested in "skyscrapers" of footnotes stretching toward the top of the page; marginalia and commentary are, for him, unwelcome appendages that should be avoided. He felt that the vision and verbal essence of the original will carry over into the target language.

Šteger wants as much of the original to cross over into English as possible, but is ultimately most concerned that the translation can function as a poem in English.

Debeljak prized accuracy but, like Šteger, was committed to the translation working as a poem in English, not minding the occasional liberty or compromise with literal meaning to achieve that.

Just as my personal relationships with each of these three people vary, my approaches to translating their poems also vary. But I always work to retain their signatures and idiosyncrasies rather than normalize or mask them.

*

Although the ideal situation would be that the translator possesses a mastery of the target and the source languages and cultures, I take some solace in John Dryden's allowance that if "a deficience" were "to be allowed in either, it is in the original" (30). In his prose poem series "Translation," Mark Strand encounters a Portuguese teacher who does not "go in for contemporary American poetry" but does not see "why that should disqualify [him] from translating." Strand's response: "You language teachers are all alike. You possess a knowledge of the original language and, perhaps, some knowledge of English, but that's it. The chances are your translations will be word-for-word renderings without the character or feel of poetry." His next remark dives into contemporary translation discourse: "You are the first to declare the impossibility of translating, but you think nothing of minimizing its difficulty" (52).

Strand is not alone in his disdain for the notion that language proficiency is the primary criterion for a translator. Burton Raffel notes that "linguistic knowledge is not the best nor even a good road toward successful translation. The translator's problems are verbal, but it is the words into which he is translating, not those from which he is taking his leave, that create his problems" (104). For Raffel, the key is that the translator possesses "the ability to manipulate and mold the receiving rather than the lending tongue" (105). And Eliot Weinberger, in "Anonymous Sources," takes this even further: "All the worst translations are done by experts in the foreign language who know little or nothing about the poetry alongside which their translations will be read" (178).

*

"Translators are the artisans of compromise." — André Lefevere, *Translating Literature* (6)

"When publishers, teachers, readers, or translators themselves require the translated text read 'as if it were written in English', as an 'elegant', 'fluent' 'good' poem 'in English,' they collude with and enforce such 'compulsory ablebodiedness.' And this is a best-case scenario, for too often publishers', teachers', and readers' anxiety over translation as an incomplete, diminished, impaired version of an original results in translation not being published, taught, or read at all." —Joyelle McSweeney and Johannes Göransson, "Manifesto of the Disabled Text"

*

Translation can be dangerous.

In Javier Marías' novella *Bad Nature, or With Elvis in Mexico*, a Spanish-born interpreter assigned to Elvis during the making of a film in Acapulco nearly gets killed for translating an insult. After a skirmish in a seedy bar, one of the members of Elvis's entourage is insulted in Spanish by the gangster-proprietors. Elvis and one of the gangsters square off, "[t]heir inability to understand each other . . . enraging them" (37). Stuck between the angry men, the translator slightly embellishes the initial insult when relaying it to Elvis (he wants to insult the man himself, albeit vicariously). Elvis's response: "You're going to repeat this word for word, Roy, to the guy with the moustache, don't you leave out one syllable" (39). Cue Elvis's insult. Elvis and his party leave, *sans* the translator, who is detained by the bad guys. One of the gangsters tells him, "you must spend a little more time with us tonight, it's early still, you can tell us about the Madre Patria and maybe even insult us some more, so we can listen to your European accent." When the translator protests, "all I did was translate," the gangster replies, "Ah, you didn't do anything but translate. . . . Too bad we don't know if that's true, we don't speak English. Whatever Elvis said we didn't understand, but you we understood, you speak very clearly . . . we heard you loud and clear, and you can rest assured that we're listening" (43).

> "[T]he translator must be responsible for her translation, for every word of it, but she cannot be held responsible for what is pledged in what she says. For she is not allowed to say what she means in what she says in translation; she is supposed to say what she says without meaning." —Naoki Sakai, *Translation and Subjectivity: On "Japan" and Cultural Nationalism* (11)

"I only had to try to get them to forgive me for words that were not mine—though they'd been on my lips, or had become real only through my lips, I was the one who had divulged them or deciphered them—but that was incredible, how could they hold me guilty for something that didn't proceed from my head or my will or my spirit. But it had come from my tongue, my tongue had made it possible, from my tongue they had grasped what was happening . . . I was the messenger, the intermediary, the translator, the true deliverer of the news . . ."
—Javier Marías, *Bad Nature, or With Elvis in Mexico* (45–46)

"No translation is ever innocent."—Alberto Manguel, *A Reader on Reading* (202)

*

In "Silence, the Devil, and Jabès," Waldrop discusses how the Brazilian poet Haroldo de Campos counters Benjamin's "There is no muse of translation" with "If translation has no muse, one could however say that it has an angel." The angel is Lucifer. This means a translation can be called a "transluciferation" (144).

Waldrop speculates that "Benjamin would have approved of the angel of light in this function since his highest claim for translation was that it allows 'the light of pure language, as though reinforced by its own medium, to shine upon the original all the more fully.'" Waldrop herself is "happy to claim Lucifer for translation as bearer of light, as the father of lies, and as the one who says 'no,' who will not serve" (144).

*

Although I believe that I am in fact translating poems from one language into another, I am always aware of the greater peril of rewriting a poem, what Weinberger warns against when he says, "Translation is dependent on the dissolution of the translator's ego for the foreign poet to enter the language—a bad translation is the insistent voice of the translator" (132). When writing my own poems, I am always conscious of fluidity and, depending on the poem, need to work toward or against it during composition. But while translating, I try (recalling A.W. Schlegel as described by Berman) neither to "modify" or "emend" rough spots nor to "embellish" the original, working to retain whatever friction or fluidity can be found in the original (131). If a poem is ungainly in Slovenian, it should be ungainly in English as well. Ditto polished, barbaric, wry, elegant, etc. A translation should not erase traces of the original.

"Obscurities *not inherent in* the matter, obscurities due not to the thing but to the wording, are a botch, and are *not* worth preserving in a translation. The work lives not by them but despite them. . . . Obscurities inherent in the thing occur when the author is piercing, or trying to pierce into, uncharted regions; when he is trying to express things not yet current, not yet worn into phrase; when he is ahead of the emotional, or philosophic sense . . . of his contemporaries." —Ezra Pound, "Translators of Greek: Early Translators of Homer" (268)

*

When translating a poem, even one that has not been translated into English yet, I rarely indulge in the illusion that I myself am writing a poem. For me, translating is a much slower process than writing. The revision and editing processes can be similar, as when I weigh various possibilities—syntactical, rhythmical, sonic—or search for the most fitting word. But, having emerged from an existing text, a translation presents a smaller set of choices. Stanzas (or the lack thereof) are set. Line logic has already been determined, as has the relationship between the poem and its title. The more radical revisions that my own poems frequently undergo—such as combining two existing poems, or cutting a 20-line poem to three lines, or transforming a sonnet into a prose poem—would feel taboo for a translation, a manifestation of the violence already implicit in the act of translation. But this is exactly what creative translation gives a poet license to do. When matters such as accuracy and fidelity are cast aside, the creative translator is free to transform the source text.

*

One of the features of translating poetry—being tethered to a source text—becomes both drawback and advantage when compared to writing poetry. When beginning a poem, I usually am looking at a blank page. Or, if I am working with a source, I radically transform it (as in erasure or collage or parody or homage). After drafting a poem, I can do great violence to the text and call it revision. I can cut most of the lines, collapse stanzas, demolish a sestina, or turn the poem on its head so that the last line becomes the first line. But I would not do such things while translating and call the result a "translation," because my imprint on the original would be so visible. (In such a case, I would be more likely to use Clive Scott's notion of "self-expressive reformulation" [72].) But this squeamishness could be a case of false modesty, since every translator utterly transforms the original text. To pretend otherwise seems willfully naive. The source is what distinguishes my traditional translations from my creative translations. When I translate poems by Šalamun, Debeljak, or Šteger, I feel an obligation to them—as both translator and friend—to carry their work into English in a way that they'll recognize as a good-faith attempt to recreate their poems in English. But when I translate poems by Rimbaud or Rilke, for example, I feel no such obligation, and the resulting poem can resemble a vandalized version more than a translation.

*

Translators of poetry, like poets, often agonize over single words. One word might convey the meaning of the original more accurately, while another might be less precise but seems more faithful to the music of the original or more sonically effective in the target language. Sometimes ambiguity in the original can push a translator to attempt to clarify or explain. Even with a long poem such as Pablo Neruda's *Alturas de Macchu Picchu*, a single word choice can cast the work into a new, perhaps even problematic light.

The themes of *Alturas de Macchu Picchu*, with its blending of indigenous and Christian values, make the poem particularly difficult to render in English because this mixture of heritages points to the paradox of identity in Latin America. The language transfer is only part of the challenge. An entire value system must be absorbed in Spanish and delivered in English for the poem to work in English. In his book *Translating Neruda: The Way to Macchu Picchu*, John Felstiner walks the reader through his decision-making processes in translating Neruda's poem. He also provides a history of Neruda translation, relevant biographical information, and his own theories of translation. Felstiner sees translation as "a process as well as a finished version," with "that process, with its origin in a strange language and culture, remaining active in the finished version" (1).

In the first five cantos of *Alturas de Macchu Picchu*, Neruda expresses the isolation, anguish, and lack of identity in urban life. He wanders through a kind of deathscape in which people die daily: "cada día una muerte pequeña," "su corta muerte diaria" (12). The horizontal movement of city life allows for no spiritual elevation. Mankind coasts on a flat spiritual plane.

But in the sixth and seventh cantos, after he has recognized the dire spiritual state of mankind, the poet ascends to Macchu Picchu on a kind of pilgrimage to his past. The dual motion—upward and downward—is necessary because as Neruda climbs to the city, he descends in time to a city buried by time. The city died "una sola muerte," "la verdadera, la más abrasadora / muerte" because its people disappeared completely (32). This collective, decisive death serves as a contrast to the individual, gradual deaths of people in the contemporary city. Neruda uses this physically and spiritually elevated vantage point to connect past to present, Macchu Picchu to modern polis.

With the Spanish Civil War behind him and World War II concurrent with his visit to Macchu Picchu, Neruda initially gives way to the temptation to look at the Peru that existed before European conquest as a sort of paradise, a world without subjugation. But he's aware of the dangers of idealizing a pre-Columbian, pre-Christian society; and in the tenth canto he implicates the Christian conquistadors in the oppression of the Latin American people.

In that canto, Neruda links the Incas to contemporary Latin Americans because, like all cities, Macchu Picchu was built on human suffering: "Macchu Picchu, pusiste / piedras en la piedra, y en la base, harapo? / Carbón sobre carbón, y en el fondo la lágrima?" (56, 58). His recognition of the oppressed/oppressor relationship in the time of Macchu Picchu illuminates the existence of class struggle, which is hardly limited to the twentieth century, even if the terminology has changed. Coming to terms with the death of an entire people allows Neruda, in the eleventh and twelfth cantos, to speak for all people in a gesture of renewal and redemption: "Yo vengo a hablar por vuestra boca muerta" (68). He joins the workers of Macchu Picchu, the workers of his day, and the reader in this spiritual transcendence through political awareness. What begins as a spiritual quest ends as a political act.

But the scope of that spirituality is debatable. As Felstiner notes in *Translating Neruda*, Nathaniel Tarn (whose translation is published by Farrar, Straus and Giroux and is thus the most widely available and widely read version of Neruda's poem) gives the poem "a more specific Christian coloring" through his translation of only three words (171). Tarn translates "panes" as "loaves" instead of the more common "bread," "relámpago" as "light" (which Felstiner thinks conjures "biblical genesis") instead of "lightning," and "vaso" as "chalice" (which Felstiner sees as "Eucharistic") instead of "vase" or "glass" (168, 175). The Christian connotation of loaves, light, and chalice (at least when compared to bread, lightning, and glass, vase, or jar) changes how the poem functions in English. Although Neruda does not avoid Christianity in the poem, he does not appear to accentuate either the Christian or the indigenous. Neruda is trying to hold together a syncretic Latin American identity that acknowledges both strains. In its attempt to marry the two strains, Tarn's translation overemphasizes the Catholic component, understates the indigenous, and seems to contradict Neruda's atheism.

Felstiner notes Tarn's dilemma here while summarizing some of the criticisms Neruda himself faced: "Neruda has been faulted for making use of his Spanish Catholic heritage while at the same time lamenting the Conquest, and no doubt that is a real split in him as in many Latin Americans. In *Alturas de Macchu Picchu*, I think he deliberately highlights neither Christian nor indigenous imagery because he is addressing a general audience, both Latin and American" (171).

The language of *Alturas de Macchu Picchu* is multitudinous: verb tenses shift, manners of address change, certain nouns contain multiple meanings, other nouns recur throughout the poem. The work is difficult to translate. As Robert Pring-

Mill notes in his preface to the Tarn edition, "Neruda works with ambiguities, not stating but suggesting, and usually suggesting a number of different lines of thought and feeling at any given time. It is this feature of his approach which makes his poetry so extraordinarily hard to translate" (xii).

Further on, Pring-Mill writes, "Ambiguous syntax is one of the most fascinating aspects of Neruda's manner of proceeding in all his complex poems, yet it is a feature which is peculiarly tantalizing to translators. They can rarely hope to establish a corresponding ambiguity, and therefore have either to opt between layers of meaning, or else to give the grammatical sense of a single layer while trying to suggest the others by words which carry heightened and conflicting associations, as Tarn does" (xii).

An English translation has to account for the many layers of Spanish without adding any new layers (such as Christian lexicon). In his own translation, Felstiner works closer to Neruda's perspective, looking beyond what the words mean to what they imply, embody, and possess. But Felstiner himself has acknowledged the interpretative aspect of translation, which he considers "the utmost case of engaged literary interpretation" (quoted in Nikolai Popov's "The Literal and the Literary," in which Popov himself writes, "translation enacts a total interpretation" [5]). Tarn's choices, then, could be a misinterpretation of Neruda's poem, or, channeling Octavio Paz ("translation implies a transformation of the original" [154]), an attempt to move the poem more firmly in one direction.

Pring-Mill, however, sees "the religious overtones" in Neruda as "quite deliberate" since they're "part of the general Catholic heritage of South America" (xiv). And the Argentinian poet Juan Larrea criticized Neruda for simultaneously Christianizing and ignoring Macchu Picchu, so it's possible that Tarn and Pring-Mill agree with Larrea's general point. Even if Neruda purposely introduced Christian overtones into the work, Tarn's three word choices place the poem squarely in a Christian tradition by infusing a non-Christian (or at least ambiguous) poem with Christian imagery. Those three words affect how English readers view the poem.

Steiner's statement in *After Babel*—"A translation is, more than figuratively, an act of double-entry; both formally and morally the books must balance"—seems apt here (319). Oddly enough, Steiner's comment recalls Dryden, who placed a premium on "maintaining the character of an author" above meaning and technical matters (24). But of course, the author's character is as open to interpretation (and as subject to translation) as meaning and technical matters are.

*

"It is translation that gives birth to the untranslatable." —Naoki Sakai, *Translation and Subjectivity: On "Japan" and Cultural Nationalism* (14)

"One does not know what one is saying, one knows after one has said it." —Maurice Merleau-Ponty, *The Prose of the World* (46)

"[T]he law of the impossibility of translation dictates that translation can occur only outside the bounds of reason and natural language." —Daniel Tiffany, *Radio Corpse* (179–80)

"Questioning the possibility of translation means to question the very possibility of literature, of writing, of language, which is always already a translation." —Pierre Joris, introduction to Paul Celan's *Breathturn* (34)

"We must not reject impossibility, but embrace it. Moments of untranslatability . . . are times for *celebration*, for not only are they privileged encounters with the foreign, but they are also opportunities for translators to ply the highest skills of their craft." —Abé Mark Nornes, "For an Abusive Subtitling" (28)

*

Most books of poetry translated from Slovenian into English come together in a certain manner. A native Slovenian speaker (often the poet) makes a literal translation, then gives it to a native English speaker, who edits the piece into a passable poem in English. Some co-translators look at the original, but most look only at the English version, which places the burden of accuracy on the person doing the literal translation and also blurs the distinction between translation and editing. To *translate*, in the conventional sense, one must *carry* something from one language to another. Strand hits upon this point in his "Translation" prose poems: "Your approach is the editorial one—you edit somebody else's translation until it sounds like yours, bypassing the most important stage in the conversion of one poem to another, which is the initial one of finding rough equivalents, one which will contain the originality of your reading" (49-50).

Paz, as we have already seen, also has addressed this: "translation implies a transformation of the original" (154). Tweaking is not transformation.

*

W.S. Merwin's *Selected Translations 1948–1968* and its sequel *Selected Translations 1968-1978* are unusual books. They include poems that he actually translated, translations of translations, composite translations of multiple translations, translations via other languages than the original, and "translations" of poems that others initially translated for him. Although he nods to these differences of approach in his forewords to the books, he does not explore how he managed the different processes, how those different processes affected the products, or why he both translated and "translated" poems and presented them the same way.

Why do these books exist in the first place? Why would we need even one volume of Merwin's *Selected Translations*—a hodgepodge that veers from language to language and across time—unless we were looking for Merwin there? The first collection includes poems from Egyptian, Chinese, Vietnamese, Kabylia, "Eskimo," Quechuan, Caxinua, Spanish, "Spanish-Jewish," Catalan, Portuguese, Italian, French, German, Romanian, Russian, Welsh, Irish, Greek, and Latin. The second includes poems from Greek, French, Spanish, Italian, Portuguese, Russian, Swedish, "American Indian," Incan, Mayan, "Eskimo" (via French versions), Japanese, Sanskrit, Persian, Turkish, and Urdu, most of them completed between 1968 and 1973, with a few more between 1974 and 1977. If Merwin had actually translated all the poems—brought them from their original languages into English—or had an over-arching plan, as Pound did, the books would constitute a towering achievement.

Compare Merwin's world tour to Pound's decades of work. (Merwin claims that Pound was the initial impetus for his translation work, so a comparison seems warranted.) Pound also translated from many languages and from different times and with varying degrees of expertise, but he was both purposeful and innovative in his approach to translation.

One might think that Merwin has sought to emulate Pound's attempt to change the poetry of his era via translation (by injecting poetry from the distant past into the present, Pound was trying to change poetry in the early twentieth century). If that was Merwin's aim, there's no evidence of it in these books of fluid translations. Merwin's own poetry, on the other hand, had a significant effect on U.S. poetry in the 1960s and 1970s. It's quite possible, of course, that his translations deeply influenced his poetry, which would make his *Selected Translations* more useful as a window onto his own poetry than as translations.

Although he claims to "approach translation as a relatively anonymous activity," says he has "not come to use translation as a way of touching off writing that then became deliberately, specially, or ostentatiously [his] own," and has "felt impelled to keep translation and [his] own writing more and more sharply separate," the editions of Merwin's *Selected Translations* read like books of Merwin poems inspired or adapted from other sources (12). And the books illustrate the risks of translating only into fluent contemporary diction, especially if the translator is also a poet who tends toward a distinctive, singular style.

In contrast, consider Pound's translations, from his early work (imitations of Guido Cavalcanti, translations of Heinrich Heine, and "The Seafarer") to 1915's *Cathay* (which includes "The River-Merchant's Wife: A Letter") to 1918's "Homage to Sextus Propertius" to his lifelong project *The Cantos* (which opens with a translation of *The Odyssey* into Anglo-Saxon meter) to his late translations—Latin translations of Confucius, a Noh rendition of Sophocles, and translations of poems by Catullus, Horace, and Rimbaud. Unlike Merwin, Pound enacts different translation strategies, so much so that translation theorists are still writing about them, some even bemoaning the fact that his modernist, anti-fluent approach to translation hadn't been more influential at the time. Ronnie Apter has discussed how Pound rejected the "pseudo-archaic diction" of Victorian era translators, using not only a contemporary diction even for old poems, but a mix of dictions, "from the genuinely archaic to the completely contemporary," sometimes within the same poem (2).

*

When I first started working with Šalamun on his poems, our process was the common one: he would do a literal translation and send the poem to me, basically for editing. This did not feel like translating to me, so I started going through the poems in the original Slovenian, translating the poems myself, comparing my versions to Šalamun's, and reconciling the two. Eventually I started translating his poems from scratch and sending him the initial translations, without his literal versions.

If I had not gone through the poems in the original, I not only wouldn't have been translating, I would have allowed some of Šalamun's typos and omissions to slip through. Some of the omissions (such as the line juxtaposing "supermodels" and "cow dung" in "Scarlet Toga" in *Woods and Chalices*) would have been particularly unfortunate.

In retrospect, beginning to translate Slovenian poetry by translating Šalamun's poems from the mid-1990s was a bit foolish. In addition to his penchant for grammatical monstrosities, Šalamun injects other languages into his poems, and he ranges across world history, literature, and geography as well as his own personal past. The poems in *Woods and Chalices* work with and off the landscape and cultural life of New York while pursuing Šalamun's multilingual, cosmopolitan perspective. (The title of the book was inspired by a view of the New York cityscape from his apartment on East 14th Street, specifically the Con Edison building and the buildings around it.) While New York is at the center of *Woods and Chalices*, the poems in the book do not remain fixed there. They fold New York into their own becoming: sometimes the city provides the setting of a poem, sometimes a launching point or simply a point of reference. His poems from this period employ rapid shifts of location, thought, image, and tone from line to line, sometimes within lines. They continue his project of breaking down and rebuilding the lyric poem. Some have described these poems as the verbal equivalent of action painting. Perhaps, but no one is trying to translate action painting.

At first, a twelve-hour work day would yield one, maybe two poems. Because I basically figured out what the poem was doing by translating it, line by line, I sometimes felt like I was playing a game, embarking on a treasure hunt to see what surprises were in store for me. "Bob Perelman is the pigeon" (40). "Poetry is a hatchery for martyrs" (24). "I grew up with eggplants" (2). "Don't sneak me onto mountains, chicken" (8). "Brooklyn, this is the skin cream" (30). Because many of Šalamun's poems resist rational thought and conventional syntax, I shifted my focus from content to the poems' basic elements, letting go of normal logic and pursuing the kind of literal translation that Šalamun supported.

Šteger's poems are something else entirely. The poems can be enigmatic or sly, but they generally stick to their subject even if they strain against it, circle it, or meander or gesture toward it. Knowing what every part of every poem was working toward helped me navigate the poems and keep moments of confusion relatively brief. (And such moments were more often due to a lack of historical or cultural context or knowledge than to gaps in the language.) Šteger employs subtle sound play, puns, allusions, and echoes in his poems; and although his poems are not formal in the traditional sense of English verse (with rhyme and meter), they possess a formal integrity that merits consideration during the translation process. The narrow, stanzaless poems in *The Book of Bodies*, for example, have a verticality and sinuousness that deserve as much attention as the words themselves. Any kind of expansion would push the poem closer to the right margin, shifting the poem's visual and rhythmical balance. Because Slovenian does not use articles, some expansion is inevitable because "the" or "a" or "an" must precede many of the nouns in the poems. When this adds a syllable, the extra weight must be counter-balanced elsewhere in the line if possible. With Šteger, the most difficult words and phrases to translate are puns and neologisms (a word, for example, that combines a popular painkiller in Slovenia with the word for "grass") and aphorisms (e.g., the Slovenian saying "to run out of potato," which means "to run out of luck," in a poem called "Potato"). In other words, the standard difficulties of translating poems.

With Šalamun, the greatest difficulties consisted of recreating an impossible statement (often formed by words being used improperly, as when nouns become verbs or a transitive verb is used intransitively, and vice versa) or figuring out how to translate a collision of multiple languages or how to convey an image that undoes itself.

In his fifties, Šalamun had become so prolific that poems would wake him in the night. This accounts for not only the vastness of his output (over fifty-five books of poetry), but also the influence of the unconscious on his poems. Like Ashbery, he had arrived at a kind of compositional freedom that came after writing thousands of poems, achieving the ability to skim the surface of the mind (impressions, images, memories) while plumbing the depths (of history, culture, myth, folklore). And like Frank O'Hara, he mentions friends by their first names alongside historical and cultural figures, some prominent, many obscure or local, with no hierarchies or distinctions.

With Debeljak's *Smugglers*, a book of sixteen-line poems (four unrhymed quatrains each) that create a psychohistorical map of Ljubljana, most of the difficulties I encountered were readily solved by some research (usually of places and historical context) or by asking Debeljak for confirmation. And I resisted smoothing out his sometimes syntactically complex

Slovenian into a simpler English, mainly because the poems' movement through personal and national history and memory resists simplification. Debeljak's poems in *Smugglers* resemble mosaics, and as such deserve to retain his distinctive blend of fluidity and intricacy.

Even though I have read every poem in Šalamun's *Woods and Chalices* at least twenty times, some of the poems still seem absolutely strange to me. Although there are few poems that I could explicate in the conventional sense, I have a relationship with most of the poems in the book. But that relationship is intuitive, process-oriented, physical.

By contrast, I have a firm grasp of Debeljak's *Smugglers* and the Šteger books that I have translated. I know what each poem is doing, how it gets where it goes, how and why it works. While discussing the poems, I could talk about process, but I also could walk someone through the poems, if not as their author, then as the closest of close readers. This is seldom possible with Šalamun's poems.

After translating one hundred poems by Šalamun, translating Šteger's *The Book of Things* seemed, mercifully at times, straightforward. My brain had received such a jolt from Šalamun that translating anything else would be like driving an actual car on an actual road, while translating Šalamun was like driving something found at a junkyard along the edge of a cliff, knowing somehow that one weren't going to crash, but not knowing where one was going, or how.

*

"One of the problems facing contemporary translation practice, and a significant inhibition when it comes to the best representation of the poet being translated, is the felt pressure in translators themselves to be original at every point, so as to distinguish their work clearly from that of previous translators of the same text. When the translation of a line or group of lines in a poem is clear—when they move easily into English in a form that is likely to occur to several different people attempting to translate them—then the assumption that the first person to translate them in this manner has somehow copyrighted them and that others must use a different form can only produce less and less effective translation. In major authors whose work is translated many times, this can become almost a principle of deteriorating translation." —David Brooks, "Srečko Kosovel: Life and Poetry" (12)

"The need to use another word in place of the more obvious, more simple, more neutral one ... may be called the *synonymizing reflex*—a reflex of nearly all translators. Having a great stock of synonyms is a feature of 'good style' virtuosity: if the word 'sadness' appears twice in the same paragraph of the original text, the translator, offended by the repetition (considered an attack on obligatory stylistic elegance), will be tempted to translate the second occurrence as 'melancholy.' But there's more: this need to synonymize is so deeply embedded in the translator's soul that he will choose a synonym first off . . ." —Milan Kundera, *Testaments Betrayed: An Essay in Nine Parts* (108)

Every translation, no matter how accurate or successful, seems provisional. If a poet's work is worth translating, then their work deserves multiple translators; and any poem that has been translated once can sustain additional translations. With some poets (Osip Mandelstam, for example), reading their work in only one translation can seem inadequate, because each translator notices and emphasizes different aspects of the work. Although I first encountered Paul Celan's work through Pierre Joris' translations and continue to prefer his translations when I read Celan, I am grateful for the translations by Michael Hamburger, John Felstiner, Ian Fairley, Jerome Rothenberg, and others because they all find different paths through the poems and make different decisions on how to carry Celan's work into English.

This stance faced a practical test when I started translating a volume of selected poems by Šalamun. I originally had planned to gather poems for the book by reprinting existing translations and adding my own translations of previously untranslated poems, but the publisher asked me to translate all the poems in the book. Because the book spans Šalamun's entire writing life, a single translator could help ensure consistency in tone, voice, syntax, and word choice. But this also meant offering alternate versions of his most well-known poems, many of which, I later learned when I started to translate previously translated poems, had been mistranslated or domesticated. The English translation of his poem "Painted Desert" in *The Four Questions of Melancholy: New and Selected Poems*, for example, is missing over 20 lines from the original. In the English translation of one of his most acclaimed poems, "History," seven lines are missing, the original poem's two stanzas have been condensed into one stanza, and some lines are out of order. The English translation of "Sand" is missing two lines that, because they repeat earlier lines, contribute to the poem's spell-like quality. Other translations add titles to untitled poems, undo repetition in the original poems, omit lines or words, contain or perpetuate typographical errors, overlook cultural or historical context, punctuate unpunctuated poems, and anglicize Slavic names. And many translations, while technically accurate, result from specific interpretations that would change with different word choices (e.g., the title of the poem "Milost" in *Poker* can be translated as "Mercy," "Pity," or "Grace," each of which affects a reading of the poem differently). All of these poems clearly benefit from multiple translations.

The most challenging aspect of retranslating Šalamun's earlier poems is recasting lines that had become well-known in English, even when the existing translation is not entirely accurate. Initially hesitant, I took some solace in the fact that Šalamun sometimes retranslated his own poems with differing results; and I recalled his preference for literal translations, a position that embraces accuracy and discourages domestication. Some of his most famous lines in English are the result of domestication, which might have been necessary to introduce a Slovenian poet to English-language readers in the 1970s and 1980s. But now that more than fifteen books by Šalamun have appeared in English translation, there is no need to translate his work in a way designed to make it more palatable to English readers. Therefore, I followed the original poems as closely as possible, even if doing so deviates from my favorite existing translations.

Rather than reprint my own translations from 2006 and 2007, I retranslated the poems, with the benefit of having translated a few books by Šteger and Debeljak in the interim. I naturally found mistakes and misunderstandings in my earlier translations, but I also found opportunities: to shift emphasis, to recast a poem's sonic scaffolding, to align a poem's lexicon with other poems in the same book, to make different syntactical connections. Even small changes to a poem can yield major differences, as when a poet revises a poem; but with retranslation, the original remains unaffected by the revision.

My 2006 translation of the poem “Meja” from Šalamun’s book *The Child and the Deer* begins:

Frontier

But you know, suffering also decays
and remains dust.
The frontier is my living body.
When a peasant burns his partridges.
It grabs. It grabs.

In my 2021 translation, I changed the title and followed the syntax and lineation of the original more closely:

The Border

But you know, suffering also decays and dust
remains.
The border is my living body.
As when a farmer heats his partridges.
Grabs. Grabs.

Because Šalamun's poems frequently scramble parts of speech, omit subjects from verbs, and embrace ambiguity, multiple translations allow for multiple readings, as in my two translations of these lines from "Meja":

The earth should cleanse itself.
It is burning up dry grass.
It removes wood and sells it. (2006)

Let the land be cleansed.
He burns dry grass.
Clears and sells wood. (2021)

The first translation casts "the earth" as the subject of the two lines following it, while the second connects the burning and logging back to the farmer. Because the original poem has three actors—the speaker, the peasant/farmer, and the earth/land—and does not always clarify who or what is behind every action, making new translations of the poem produces fundamental differences that essentially become new poems.

*

In César Aira's novella *The Literary Conference*, an out-of-work translator also happens to be a mad scientist bent on world domination. The crux of his plan to take over the world is to clone (I initially typed "quote") a genius—the Mexican writer Carlos Fuentes.

Thus the translator *clones* the genius.

But things go awry when the mad scientist snicks a cell from Fuentes' silk tie, not Fuentes himself, and inserts it in the cloning machine. The result: enormous silkworms that threaten to destroy the city.

Thus the translator merely clones the genius's garmenture.

*

“‘Translation’ is too mild a word to capture the violent process whereby a text written in one language and time is taken apart and rebuilt in another. Perhaps ‘metamorphosis’ comes closer.” —Frederick Ahl, “*Uilix Mac Leirtis*: The Classical Hero in Irish Metamorphosis” (173)

“One translates in order to possess.” —Burton Raffel, *The Forked Tongue* (15)

*

In Linh Dinh's short story "Prisoner with a Dictionary" in *Blood and Soap*, a prisoner's only possession is a dictionary in a language he does not know. After using the book for various purposes—stool, pillow, toilet paper—he decides to learn the language, even though "each definition was made up of words entirely unknown to him" (1). So an unknown word would lead him to other unknown words. Nevertheless, he remains "determined to memorize every definition on every page" (2). His acquisition of the new language causes him to forget "nearly all the words of his native language" (3).

"Although he did not know what the words meant, what they referred to in real life, he reasoned that he *understood* these words because he knew their definitions. And because he was living inside this language all the time, like a fetus thriving inside a womb, there were times when he felt sure he could guess at the general implications of a word . . . But his guesses were always wrong, of course" (2).

So the prisoner becomes a translator. In the end, "the only word he ever acquired for sure was 'dictionary,' simply because it was printed on the cover of a book he knew for sure was a dictionary. [And] even as he ran across the definition for 'prisoner,' and was memorizing it by heart, he didn't even know that he was only reading about himself" (4).

*

In Šalamun's poem "The Wood's White Arm," I initially translated "Nathan's headboard is in Prague" as "Nathan's bedhead is in Prague," because the Slovenian phrase literally means "head of bed." I puzzled over "bedhead" for a little while—how someone's unkempt hair could be in Prague, ostensibly separate from the person whose hair it is— until I realized (with some help from Google image search, which presented me with scores of photographs of hotel rooms) that the correct term is "headboard." I was simultaneously amused at my error and relieved at correcting it. And then, when I looked at the corrected line, I felt confused all over again.

*

"One is, of necessity, more sensitive to botches in one's own tongue than to botches in another, however carefully learned." —Ezra Pound, "Translators of Greek: Early Translators of Homer" (264)

"I see the poet-translator in the service of the original, not attempting to improve on it or to outwit it." —Clayton Eshleman, "At the Locks of the Void" (143)

"Translation should embody an act of thanks to the original. It should celebrate its own dependence on its source." —George Steiner, "Marrow versus marrow" (9)

*

Translation is central to all acts of writing. Consider the German Romantic Novalis' assertion (quoted in Berman's *The Experience of the Foreign*) that "In the final analysis, all poetry is translation" (14). And the French poet Paul Valéry: "Writing anything at all . . . is a work of translation exactly comparable to that of transmuting a text from one language into another" (116). As Steiner points out in *After Babel*, we already engage in an act of translation—specifically intralingual diachronic translation—when reading literature from the past, because language, "in perpetual change," "is the most salient model of Heraclitean flux. It alters at every moment in perceived time" (18). And sensibilities and mores also change, adding another layer of difference: "When we read or hear any language-statement from the past, . . . we translate" (28). The translation occurs across time. So the issue of translation does not need to be limited to crossing from one language to another; its vocabularies and strategies and concerns also apply to writing and reading within one's own language.

Even if we remain in the present, we can tap into the otherness embedded in English, not simply for aesthetic reasons, but to achieve what French theorist Antoine Berman advocates as "the very aim of translation—to open up in writing a certain relation with the Other, to fertilize what is one's Own through the mediation of what is Foreign." A translational approach to writing marks writing as "an opening, a dialogue, a cross-breeding, a decentering," a site of engagement, not of entrenchment (4).

In her piece "Middling English," Caroline Bergvall seems to agree:

> The dispersed, intensely regional transformations of English active in the Middle English of Chaucer's days are again to be found in the inventive and adaptive, dispersed, diversely anglo-mixed, anglo-phonic, anglo-foamic languages practiced around the world today, as they follow or emerge from the grooves of military, commercial, cultural transport and trafficking. This transport flows across both diachronic and synchronic routes . . . (14)

In their discussion of Kafka, Deleuze and Guattari praise the writer who can "make use of the polylingualism of one's own language, . . . make a minor or intensive use of it" (26-27). Here we have "a becoming-minor of the major language," which requires "absolute deterritorialization" (26). Kafka "submits German to creative treatment as a minor language, constructing a continuum of variation" and wants "to make language stammer, or make it 'wail,' stretch tensors through all of language, . . . and draw from it cries, shouts, pitches, durations, timbres, accents, intensities" (*A Thousand Plateaus* 104). The goal is to "use the minor language to *send the major language racing*," to "bring language slowly and progressively to the desert" (*Kafka* 26). This is akin to what Bergvall calls "the meddle": "denaturalization of one's personal and cultural premise" (14).

This notion of a minor literature composed within a major language can be applied to poetry in English. Because poetry is marginal and marginalized, poets are already working in a minor register. And if we accept Valéry's definition of the language of poetry—that poetry is a separate language within a language—then we could argue that poetry automatically constitutes a minor literature and that its status as such should be cultivated rather than undone through concessions to mainstream and dominant modes of discourse.

But why not go further, and destabilize the language in the way advocated by Deleuze and Guattari? The French linguist Jean-Jacques Lecercle speaks of the "pleasurable violence" (66) that we can inflict upon language, which we can connect to Philip E. Lewis' notion of strategically abusive translations—"the strong, forceful translation that values experimentation, tampers with usage . . ." (226).

This is where translation—as an activity and as a way of thinking about writing—can help us broaden our sense of poetry. Many translators and philosophers have addressed the necessity for translation to work upon the target language at least as much as the source language. Rudolf Pannwitz, as quoted in Berman's *The Experience of the Foreign*, has noted that "The fundamental error of the translator is to preserve the contingent state of his own language rather than submit it to the violent motion of the foreign language" (18). Just as poetry exerts pressure on the language in which it's written, translations should seek to reshape their target language. Poets like Robert Browning, Friedrich Hölderlin and Pound have shown how one can do this both ways—via translation *and* original composition. Their translations blend target and source languages to create a kind of interlingua, "a centaur-idiom" (Steiner 332).

Consider the singular case of Armand Schwerner, whose epic *The Tablets* purports to be a translation of ancient Sumero-Akkadian texts rendered and annotated by a "Scholar/Translator." The texts, of course, are of Schwerner's own invention, yet the methods and apparatus of translation give him opportunities for innovation that would not exist otherwise.

Translation of poetry occurs along a spectrum of fluency and resistancy, or domestication and foreignization. In 1813 Freidrich Schleiermacher claimed that the translator could move the original author toward the reader (domestication) or bring the reader to the author (foreignization). Fluent, domesticating translation strives for transparency and effaces the status of the translation as a translation. Resistant, foreignizing translation works against the dominant mode of the receiving language and implements strategies that call attention to themselves because they refuse transparency. Innovative contemporary poetry is inherently resistant, seeking discontinuity rather than fluidity, opacity rather than transparency, parataxis rather than hypotaxis, incompletion rather than coherence.

I am especially interested in ways of using translation to expand the sense of what's possible in writing, to go beyond (without rejecting) currently fashionable techniques of parataxis, ostranenie, language games, syntactic dislocations, and heightened artifice, in the spirit of Ilya Kaminsky's statement from his introduction to *The Ecco Anthology of International Poetry*: translation shows us "the genius of what is possible in English, as it bends each single one of its own rules to accommodate various new forms. We learn something new about the English language each time we confront another syntax, another grammar, another musical way of organizing silences in a mouth. By translating, we learn how the limits of our English-speaking minds can be stretched to accommodate the foreign . . ." (xl).

Alternative translation practices can elicit resistancy in the target language, while also calling forth what Lecercle describes as the "remainder"—that which exceeds the needs of communication and focuses our attention on the process and medium of communication (5). The remainder appears in dialects, idiolects, archaisms, neologisms, nonsense, bar-

barities, puns, slogans, and jargon. So the remainder also contains an element of instability and corruption, in which a dead language feeds off a living language while also giving it life: "The first rule of the remainder is the rule of *exploitation* . . . in language all rules . . . can be defeated and give rise to exploitation. This is where the remainder is negative and subversive, locked in endless combat with tendencies towards order" (122). The remainder is "unchecked by the constraints of reference or systematic rationality" (66).

I am also interested in work composed in English that foreignizes itself, works within the remainder to access the foreign within the familiar. Values and strategies of decentering, confrontation, hybridization in translation, which work at the levels of language and culture, can provide a different way for poets to contextualize their work, to consider audience in larger ways.

In a way, this nods to Deleuze and Guattari's notion of a minor utilization of a major language—or a minor literature composed within a major language: for example, Kafka, or Celan, whose work deterritorializes German, actively works against the dominant mode of the language. Now if we're writing poetry in English, clearly a major language, we're already automatically working in a minor register, because poetry is marginal and marginalized. But to go further, our use of English would need to destabilize the language.

Homophonic translation is probably the clearest route to achieve this. But there are other translation-esque techniques that can release this remainder: erasures and treatments like Ronald Johnson's *RADI OS* or Jen Bervin's *Nets*. These works are most effective when, like traditional translations, they create a new space between the original and the new version, altering the original as well as the translation, confront hidden elements in the original, and exert pressure on English.

Erasures are reminiscent of translation practices, such as that of the German Romantics, which consciously appropriated other literatures and texts to build their own. As Berman has noted, in Germany there is "a tradition of translation that regards translation as the creation, transmission, and expansion of the language," and thus of the culture (27). "The formulation and the development of a national culture of its own can and must proceed by way of translation, that is, by an intensive and deliberate relation to the foreign" (32). It's through "alienation, in the strictest sense of the word, that a relation to oneself is possible" (32). Given the colonizing tendencies of U.S. culture and of the English language, such an exposure to otherness seems not only aesthetically compelling, but urgent.

Other translational possibilities for writing include:

> excavation, digging into the language to reclaim parts of it;
>
> new media poetries that unsettle the stability of an original text while transforming it;
>
> multilingual and multi-discourse writing—archaic, colloquial, scientific, etc.—that not only works against the dominant poetic mode (first-person lyric), but also cultivates the otherness and multiplicity inherent in English, resists literary and cultural norms, attempts to recover "the excluded and the marginal" (Venuti 177), and avoids assimilation and transparency;

nonsense and neologisms, which can remind readers of the constructedness of what they're reading, of the process of making meaning;

appropriation, or what Marjorie Perloff in her book *Unoriginal Genius* terms "citationality" and "its dialectic of removal and graft, disjunction and conjunction, its interpenetration of origin and destruction" (17), as well as treating quotation as what Clive Scott describes as "extremely close translation," which posits that "any recontextualization of a text . . . is to make it something new. . . . an original text does not need to be translated in order to be 'translated'; it simply needs another environment" (126).

*

I cannot know precisely how Šteger's poems strike a native Slovenian speaker, but in English, the poems simultaneously carry weight and move lightly. They seem both immense and feathery. And the poems have changed how I view some things—urinals, graters, and umbrellas especially. Šteger himself was the first translator of *The Book of Things*, carrying the poems from the land of objects into language. I simply recreated them in another language. Šteger established equivalencies between things and words; I established equivalencies between words and words.

*

If Šalamun translates ones of his poems from the original Slovenian to English, are we sure that the original version is the Slovenian poem? Could the original be a combination of Slovenian and English, with the Slovenian version serving as an initial (albeit published) draft? When someone else translates the poem from Slovenian to English, we can be more confident saying that the original is the poem in Slovenian because no English version of the poem existed before. But if the author brings the poem into existence in two languages, in whatever order, how can we say with certainty that the original version is necessarily the first?

> "A peculiarly illuminating, intentional strangeness can result when a writer, particularly a lyric writer, translates his own work into a foreign language or is instrumental in such translation." —George Steiner, *After Babel* (336)

*

Šalamun's position on translation is the opposite of Benjamin's belief that the "literal rendering of the syntax completely demolishes the theory of reproduction of meaning and is a direct threat to comprehensibility" (79). Of course, when a poet's own work is "a direct threat to comprehensibility," it seems appropriate that the translation advances that aim, too.

The primary temptation while working with Šalamun's poetry is to employ translation as a method of interpretation or, worse, domestication, simplification, or clarification. Rather than reproduce a phrase or line or sentence literally (which sometimes produces a statement that makes no conventional sense), the translator might want to adjust the phrase or line or sentence so that it makes sense. Because a translator has to make choices constantly, the risk of imposing an interpretation—of trying to figure out the meaning of a syntactical unit that might have no rational meaning, and then inserting the conclusions into the translation—is constant. But the translator needs to resist resolving ambiguities in the original.

*

Because I focus intently on the line when I write poems, while translating I work to maintain the original poem's lineation in English. But the Slovenian poets that I've translated have different attitudes toward the line, compelling me to adjust and expand my view of how a poetic line can function.

Šalamun viewed the beginnings of lines as more important than the endings (thus the prevalence of traditionally weak line breaks in his work). During an email conversation about his lines and line breaks, he wrote, "I usually 'rime' at the beginning of the line, not at the end, therefore these strange cuttings of lines." This compelled me to balance my own preference for strong line endings with his preference for strong beginnings while working to maintain the logic of his lines.

If a line is getting unwieldy in translation, extending too far beyond its neighbors, Šteger welcomes moving a phrase down to the next line, thus breaking the original line and the integrity of that line for the sake of overall balance within the poem.

Debeljak was even more concerned with the visual appearance of the line. He wanted the lengths of the lines of the poems in *Smugglers* to match as closely as possible because he conceived the poems as a grid. For him, the form of each poem in the book becomes a vessel to be filled with memories and associations. Thus, the formal integrity or logic of individual lines can be sacrificed for the sake of that visual symmetry. One of my tasks, then, was to reconcile his fondness for symmetry with my own commitment to the line as a poetic unit.

While translating *Woods and Chalices,* I often asked Šalamun about lines and line breaks and also tried to explain my choices. In an email from July 21, 2006, I wrote:

> "I've noticed in general that your line breaks in the original tend to disappear in your English versions, probably because you're working to maintain relatively even lines throughout the English version. I'd like to maintain as many of the significant line breaks as possible while paying attention to that evenness and to the possibilities of enjambment and soundplay in English. So when I notice something in the Slovenian, I try to bring it over into English; and when it doesn't mar the English version or skew the original to introduce a little electricity of form, I do so. An example is the first stanza of this poem:
>
> > The fullness whispers, fragrant. It spreads the nose
> > and rolls up the skin. My fins grow and flutter—flags—,
> > with my finger I touch an elbow, to test if it hears
>
> "Ending the first line with 'nose' and the third line with 'hears' offers a resonant but quiet rhyme. Ending the second line with 'flags' and the dash followed by a comma maintains the abruptness of the phrase but also becomes a flag of its own within the line and stanza. Also, ending the third line with 'hears' creates a strong enjambment because the reader doesn't know the object of 'hears' until they go to the next stanza—so it's an enjambment that furthers both form and content.

“There’s similar work in the second stanza—‘circle’ and ‘frills’ have a quiet chime, and ‘milkier’ bridges the two with its own ‘k’ and ‘L’ sounds while working with the same sounds in the other words in that stanza.

“I just wanted to give you a sense of what I’m trying to do with your lines—respecting the original as much as possible while putting pressure on the English.”

*

When the poet wants the translated poems to function in English as poems in English (i.e., when the poet expressly asks for a fluid translation), I have been more willing to sacrifice some meaning in the original to make the poem work as an English-language poem. But the translated poem should always contain a certain amount of strangeness—not exoticized foreignness, but a reminder that the poem originated elsewhere. Translators need to resist English's tendency to absorb everything. However important a poet like Šalamun is to American poetry readers, his work cannot and should not be Americanized.

With Šalamun, I emphatically wanted the poems to seem peculiar in English. To do otherwise would have been to compromise the real substance of his poems. With Šteger and Debeljak, I worked to make the poems read well in English, but maintained as many of the poems' idiosyncrasies as possible rather than try to normalize or erase them. For example, I preserved the proliferation of commas in *Smugglers* when English usage would call for periods, semi-colons, and/or dashes. And I carried the peculiarities of the poem "Hayrack" in *The Book of Things* into English, particularly in the neologism "morphield," which corresponds with the Slovenian neologism "travmal" in the original text ("travmal" combines the Slovenian word for "grass" with the name of a popular analgesic, Tramal), and in the poem's litany of imaginary military figures from countries bordering Slovenia: Brigadiere Hayrackino, Hauptmann Hayracker, Ezredes Häyräckek, and Pukovnik Hayrakić.

*

Ten years before I started translating, I asked the Irish poet Nuala Ní Dhomhnaill what was most important to her when her poems crossed over into English. Her answer: "voltage." Not literal meaning, not the basic gist, not the form, not music. Voltage.

Ní Dhomhnaill was reiterating what she had said in a conversation with Medbh McGuckian published in *The Southern Review* in 1995: "The most important thing is to get the voltage that is behind the words" (61). My *Webster's* defines *voltage* as "electromotive force or potential difference expressed in volts." If we say that the volt is the equivalent of the word, then voltage can become the "electromotive force or potential difference expressed" in words. Potential difference is "the difference between the potentials of two points in an electric field, equal to the amount of work done in moving a relatively small charge from one point to the other." If we consider the "electric field" to be language itself, the two points become the two languages (source and target), where the transference of energy from one point to another becomes a transference of language and all that it embodies culturally, socially, historically, and ontologically. But let's not forget "electromotive," "pertaining to, producing, or tending to produce a flow of electricity." If we accept language as a dynamic electric field, the process of translation becomes electromotive in that it pertains to and produces a flow of electricity—a flow of language that relies on voltage for its impact. But with translation, we cannot measure or assign a specific value to the flow of words from one language to another. Ní Dhomhnaill's voltage, because it's word-driven, is indefinable.

". . . the retina is made up of special cells called rods and cones. These cells change the light that falls on them. The pattern of light becomes a pattern of nerve signals going to the brain. 'It's like translating one language into another,' said Tim. 'The rods and cones translate "light language" into "nerve language."'" —*The Magic School Bus Explores the Senses* (15)

*

While working Šalamun's poems into English, I felt like I was fully alert, my senses open to all stimuli. I felt inspired, creative. I knew that I was writing a poem and that I myself was writing nothing. Berman captures this paradox in *The Experience of the Foreign*: the translator "presents himself as a writer, but is only a re-writer. He is an author, but never The Author" (5). But there's also Maurice Blanchot in *Friendship*: ". . . the man who is ready to translate is in a constant, dangerous and admirable intimacy—and it is this familiarity that gives him the right to be the most arrogant or the most secret of writers—with the conviction that, in the end, translating is madness" (61).

> "[T]he impossibility lodged within translation is itself death, madness—and originality." —Daniel Tiffany, *Radio Corpse* (187)

> "The translator is a writer of singular originality, precisely where he seems to claim none." —Maurice Blanchot, *Friendship* (59)

> "Verse translation at its best generates a wholly new utterance in the second language—new, yet equivalent, of equal value." —John Felstiner, *Translating Neruda* (27)

*

"In line 4 [of 'The Linden Tree'], does the lightning 'report from' heaven or 'report on' (or 'tell on' / 'tattle on') heaven? The idea of lightning reporting 'from' heaven seems tamer than lightning reporting/telling 'on' heaven. Also, lightning could be seen as an indicator of heaven's whereabouts, thus giving it away, giving its secret location away."
—Brian Henry to Tomaž Šalamun, July 22, 2006

"[A] translator moves between two extremes, neither settling for literalism nor leaping into improvisation, but somehow shaping a poem that is likewise inalienable and organic." —John Felstiner, *Translating Neruda* (30)

*

Once, trying to understand part of a Šalamun poem ("Fallow Land and the Fates"), I wrote to him with some questions, beginning with my rough translation of the poem, with alternatives in brackets:

The Fallow [Fallow Land? Virgin Soil?] and the Fates

The boy scrubs the kitchen and crushes [crumbles?] mommy's
period. Godfathers ignite
microwaves. Snakes, Easter eggs,
gray hats and crampon lamps
flake from columns [pillars?] in walls.
He who brews brandy pants around scree,
incantation. He who boils carries [Boils he who carries?] the
mountain
and this one, who unsaddles supports yuppies.
I turn [rotate?] breasts [chest?] and papers. The river makes
the bow [ribbon?]. It's easy to find shapes in the profiles
of stones, but in the mud there's the weight
of the horse-collar. [Stools], you sink because
you don't penetrate [prick?] the water. Only the shattered
water drinks water. The full [crowded? stuffed?] water twists.

Is "fallow" in the title an adjective or a noun? "fallow" cannot exist as a noun in English without "land" following it, so if it's a noun, the title should be "Fallow Land and the Fates."

In the title, what are other possible meanings for "parke" (other than "park")?

Any alternatives for "piko"? since it is also a full stop, can we use "period" instead? or does that possibly skew the meaning by alluding to the mother's menstruation? I'm not satisfied with "dot" because the image of crushing/crumbling a dot doesn't make sense as it is written.

Is "luščijo" in line 4 being used as a verb or a noun? if a verb, it should come at the end of the sentence and be "flake" (I am guessing the image is pillars on walls with those things on them flaking or peeling off). If a noun, it should come at the beginning and be "husk": "husks of snakes, Easter eggs, . . ."

In the last line, is "voda" "polna" because it's full from drinking, or is it full of other things? if it's not full from drinking water, we should use "crowded" or maybe "stuffed."

Does the person who makes the liquor boil the person who carries the mountain? or should those be different people?

Can you explain the action behind "Obračam prsi in papirje"?

—Brian Henry to Tomaž Šalamun, July 20, 2006

His reply:

Zdrobiti piko mamici means exactly to crush the dot to mom. Let's leave it.

As if mother would have a dot and the son would crush it. Of course the dot is not corporeal and we couldn't crush it and why the mom would have a dot and how would that look like we don't know and cannot imagine. This is the clue for my writing. This is the disturbing part that it makes no sense. *Pika* here is a dot, not period. There's a possible subconscious English perversion, but it should stay hidden. Period would destroy everything here. The fact that it doesn't make sense makes it a line.

The godfathers didn't ignite microwaves, microwaves started to burn by themselves as if they were paper or logs and it happened to godfathers. Maybe also: Microwaves got on fire to the godfathers.

Sopsti po melishchih is utterly weird in Slovenian, it should stay like this, "around scree" I feel as logifying, better is "on screes." "On" is more physical, the fact that it happens on many screes not only to one is more interesting. I'm a destroyer of images, I don't make images, I block them deep in the ground.

In the tenth line I propose "tie" or "mesh," because "bow" could mean the river bows. "Ribbon" would escape too close to the sense that the river makes ribbons with its flowing. My image is much more radical. The river makes a mesh.

Please leave "Sinking stools, you can't pierce water!" Maybe the exclamation point is missing. The stools are sinking and I'm telling them that they cannot pierce water. That's all. They're sinking already, we cannot add because etc. Don't try to tame my crystal madness. Things are completely simple. I only describe what they do or they do what I order them to do. And they like to do what was not done before.

*

After going through Šalamun's "The King Likes the Sun" a few times, I found what I thought was a problem:

Looking at the poem again, I noticed a problem with the three *its* in the first four lines.

> In the line "It opens like a patch", does "it" refer to the invention? If so, we have an antecedent problem, because "it" is used twice before to refer to the people's request (or to the people, I'm not sure). I also wonder if "it" refers to the empire, which immediately follows; though this wouldn't make sense in English, I could see it working in Slovenian, since grammatical effects are different.
>
> We can solve this by changing "it" in "He didn't overlook it" and "He wasn't able to overlook it" to "them" and keep "It opens like a patch." That would make the "it" referring to the invention pretty clear.
>
> How does that sound?
>
> I've changed "wrapper" to "wrap" because "wrap" is used for clothing and "wrapper" is not. I also like the effect of the monosyllables there.
>
> Also, another good reason for blisters instead of calluses is that blisters come first, before calluses.
>
> I also propose changing "obtains" in the line "the pole obtains azure" because "obtains" is really awkward.
>
> —Brian Henry to Tomaž Šalamun, July 22, 2006

His response:

> I like wrap instead of wrapper, but for all the other changes I'm not.
>
> I don't see a problem if there's a lot of ambiguity. They have to be. Some sentences walk in the mist, some bend strangely, I like awkwardness, awkwardness is the crucial thing in my writing. Things should not be clear. If clear they're too domesticated. I dedomesticate, invade the language, delogify. My sentences should take off the sense of balance, not to repeat the words too much is a French classicist law. I don't see it as a problem. Third it refers to invention, fourth to empire (maybe) but exactly that you don't really know is what I like and deliberately do.
>
> —Tomaž Šalamun to Brian Henry, July 24, 2006

And a postscript:

> Exactly the fact that first are blisters which become calluses is the reason that I say First are calluses, I function through paradox, negativity, opposites. Blisters is too normal and elegant, calluses are heavier, inelegant.
>
> The pole goes azure is too normal. The pole obtains azure dark water surface. This is how it should be, it is exactly what I say. Maybe the comma in Slovenian confuses you that you make two different parts. The comma in Slovenian is ambivalent, it wants to slightly confuse.
>
> —Tomaž Šalamun to Brian Henry, July 24, 2006

*

On the rare occasion, I have created more complexity than existed in the original. In Debeljak's "Balkan Bridge," for example, I translated the phrase "v vsakem naključju počiva ključ" as "a coin in every coincidence" (52-53). In the original, "ključ" literally means "key" (not "coin") and "naključju" means "coincidence," "chance," or "accident." Because of the way in which "ključ" is embedded within "naključju," I wanted to achieve the same effect in English. Although they seem unrelated, "key" and "coin" share a few poetic elements: both are monosyllabic words, both begin with the "k" sound, and a coin can function as a kind of key, unlocking a washing machine or arcade game or pay phone, and "coin" can open doors in society. (Whoever has enough coin can unlock any door.) Debeljak noticed that I had not translated that word literally, but he also recognized what I had done with "ključ" and "naključju," writing "it invalidates my private claim that there's a key in every coincidence only in Slovenian," and "This I cherish extra!"

For me, translating poems can resemble a kind of puzzle, in that my brain is as occupied with *solving* something—not an equation, but perhaps an equivalency—as it is with fashioning a poem in English from a poem in Slovenian.

*

"In translation the original rises into a higher and purer linguistic air, as it were. It cannot live there permanently, to be sure, and it certainly does not reach it in its entirety. Yet, in a singularly impressive manner, at least it points the way to this region: the predestined, hitherto inaccessible realm of reconciliation and fulfillment of languages. The transfer can never be total, but what reaches this region is that element in a translation which goes beyond transmittal of subject matter. This nucleus is best defined as the element that does not lend itself to translation." —Walter Benjamin, "The Task of the Translator" (76)

But . . .

". . . the language of the translation envelops its content like a royal robe with ample folds. For it signifies a more exalted language than its own and thus remains unsuited to its content, overpowering and alien." —Walter Benjamin, "The Task of the Translator" (76)

*

"I'm very very conservative about translations. I believe in purity and accurateness, the translator should never intervene with his ego, he (she) should just listen carefully, not adding his (her) own inventions if they don't burst by the text itself. I never believed in homophonic translations, it's just a bad shadow of 'fun' American ideology for me." —Tomaž Šalamun to Brian Henry, January 30, 2011

While the writer need follow no rules, the translator is obliged to follow the rules—or at least the blueprints—laid down by the writer in the work being translated. Even if the writer is unconventional or wildly innovative, their work establishes new conventions that necessarily restrain the translator.

"A real translation is transparent; it does not cover the original, does not block its light, but allows the pure language, as though reinforced by its own medium, to shine upon the original all the more fully. This may be achieved, above all, by a literal rendering of the syntax which proves words rather than sentences to be the primary element of the translator" —Walter Benjamin, "The Task of the Translator" (79–0)

With poetry, Valéry says, "fidelity to meaning alone is a kind of betrayal. How many poetic works, reduced to prose, that is, to their simple meaning, become literally nonexistent! They are anatomical specimens, dead birds! . . . Verse is put into prose as though into its coffin" (116).

*

Rather than be worked upon by the target language, the source language works on, leaks into, changes the target language.

So much of the rhetoric about poetry translation centers not just on impossibility, but on loss. Rather than focus on what is lost in translation, let's look at what can be carried over: most of a poem's literal meaning, its tone and atmosphere, some of its music (including a comparable sonic scaffolding), much of its attitude and vision. This isn't everything, clearly, but it's certainly better than nothing.

There's no reason to let the "unavoidable imperfection in all translations" (Schopenhauer 32) impoverish our literature. If, as Yves Bonnefoy claims, "a poem is less than poetry," what is lost at the level of the individual poem is more than compensated for by what is added to the art of poetry (187). In a way, the individual poem sacrifices itself—is sacrificed—for the sake of the art as a whole.

Works Cited

Ahl, Frederick. "*Uilix Mac Leirtis*: The Classical Hero in Irish Metamorphosis." *The Art of Translation: Voices from the Field*, edited by Rosanna Warren, Northeastern UP, 1989, pp. 173–98

Aira, César. *The Literary Conference*. Translated by Katherine Silver, New Directions, 2010.

Apter, Ronnie. *Digging for the Treasure: Translation after Pound*. Peter Lang, 1984.

Benjamin, Walter. "The Task of the Translator." Translated by Harry Zohn. *Theories of Translation: An Anthology of Essays from Dryden to Derrida*, edited by Rainer Schulte and John Biguenet, U of Chicago P, 1992, pp. 71–82.

Bergvall, Caroline. *Meddle English: New and Selected Texts*. Nightboat Books, 2010.

Berman, Antoine. *The Experience of the Foreign: Culture and Translation in Romantic Germany*. Translated by S. Heyvaert, SUNY P, 1992.

Bernstein, Charles. "Breaking the Translation Curtain: The Homophonic Sublime." *Towards a Foreign Likeness Bent: Translation*, edited by Jerrold Shiroma, Duration, 2005, pp. 10–12.

Blanchot, Maurice. *Friendship*. Translated by Elizabeth Rottenberg, Stanford UP, 1997.

Bonnefoy, Yves. "Translating Poetry." Translated by John Alexander and Clive Wilmer. *Theories of Translation: An Anthology of Essays from Dryden to Derrida*, edited by Rainer Schulte and John Biguenet, U of Chicago P, 1992, pp. 186–92.

Borges, Jorge Luis. *This Craft of Verse*. Harvard UP, 2000.

Brooks, David. "Srečko Kosovel: Life and Poetry." *The Golden Boat* by Srečko Kosovel, Salt Publishing, 2008.

Cole, Joanna. *The Magic School Bus Explores the Senses*. Scholastic, 2001.

Debeljak, Aleš. *Smugglers*. Translated by Brian Henry, BOA Editions, 2015.

Deleuze, Gilles. *The Logic of Sense*. Translated by Mark Lester with Charles Stivale, Columbia UP, 1990.

Deleuze, Gilles and Félix Guattari. *Kafka: Toward a Minor Literature*. Translated by Dana Polan, U of Minnesota P, 1986.

—. *A Thousand Plateaus*. Translated by Brian Massumi, U of Minnesota P, 1987.

Dinh, Linh. *Blood and Soap*. Seven Stories P, 2004.

Dryden, John. "On Translation." *Theories of Translation: An Anthology of Essays from Dryden to Derrida*, edited by Rainer Schulte and John Biguene, U of Chicago P, 1992, pp. 17–32.

Eshleman, Clayton. *Companion Spider: Essays*. Wesleyan UP, 2001.

Felstiner, John. *Translating Neruda: The Way to Macchu Picchu*. Stanford UP, 1980.

Gass, William. *Reading Rilke: Reflections on the Problems of Translation*. Alfred A. Knopf, 1999.

Gavronsky, Serge. "The Translation: From Piety to Cannibalism," *SubStance*, vol. 16, 1977, pp. 53–62.

Göransson, Johannes. "The Immigrant Is Transposition Kitsch." *Exoskeleton*, 2010, http://exoskeleton-johannes.blogspot.com/2010/03/fashionismtranslationtransposition.html.

Hawkey, Christian. *Ventrakl*. Ugly Duckling Presse, 2010.

Hejinian, Lyn. *The Language of Inquiry*. U of California P, 2000.

Joris, Pierre. Introduction to *Breathturn* by Paul Celan. Sun and Moon P, 1995.

Kaminsky, Ilya. "Introduction." *The Ecco Anthology of International Poetry*. Ecco P, 2010.

Kundera, Milan. *Testaments Betrayed: An Essay in Nine Parts*. Translated by Linda Asher, HarperCollins, 1995.

Lecercle, Jean-Jacques. *The Violence of Language*. Routledge, 1990.

Lefevere, André. "Mother Courage's Cucumbers: Text, System and Refraction in a Theory of Literature." *The Translation Studies Reader*, edited by Lawrence Venuti, Routledge, 2012.

—. *Translating Literature: Practice and Theory in a Comparative Literature Context*. Modern Language Association, 1992.

Lewis, Phillip E. "The Measure of Translation Effects." *The Translation Studies Reader*, edited by Lawrence Venuti, Routledge, 2012, pp. 220–39.

Manguel, Alberto. *A Reader on Reading*. Yale UP, 2010.

Marías, Javier. *Bad Nature, or With Elvis in Mexico*. Translated by Esther Allen, New Directions, 2010.

McSweeney, Joyelle, and Johannes Göransson. "Manifesto of the Disabled Text." *Exoskeleton*, 2008, http://exoskeleton-johannes.blogspot.com/2008/06/manifesto-of-disabled-text.html.

Merleau-Ponty, Maurice. *The Prose of the World*. Translated by John O'Neill, Northwestern UP, 1973.

Merwin, W. S. *Selected Translations*. Copper Canyon P, 2013.

Middleton, Christopher. "Translation as a Species of Mime." *The Art of Translation: Voices from the Field*, edited by Rosanna Warren, Northeastern UP, 1989, pp. 21–29.

Nabokov, Vladimir. "Problems of Translation." *Theories of Translation: An Anthology of Essays from Dryden to Derrida*, edited by Rainer Schulte and John Biguenet, U of Chicago P, 1992, pp. 127–43.

Neruda, Pablo. *The Heights of Macchu Picchu: A Bilingual Edition*. Translated by Nathaniel Tarn, Farrar, Straus and Giroux, 1967.

Ní Dhomhnaill, Nuala, and Medbh McGuckian. "Comhra, with a Foreword and Afterword by Laura O'Connor." *The Southern Review*, vol.31, no. 3, 1995, pp. 581–614.

Nornes, Abé Mark. "For an Abusive Subtitling." *Film Quarterly*, vol. 52, no. 3, 1999, pp. 17–34.

Paz, Octavio. "Translation: Literature and Letters." Translated by Irene del Corral. *Theories of Translation: An Anthology of Essays from Dryden to Derrida*, edited by Rainer Schulte and John Biguenet U of Chicago P, 1992, pp. 152–62.

Perloff, Marjorie. *Unoriginal Genius*. U of Chicago P, 2010.

Popov, Nikolai. "The Literal and the Literary." *The Iowa Review*, vol. 32, no. 3, 2002, pp. 1–25.

Pound, Ezra. "Translators of Greek: Early Translators of Homer." *Literary Essays of Ezra Pound*, edited by T. S. Eliot, New Directions, 1935, pp. 249–75.

Raffel, Burton. *The Forked Tongue: A Study of the Translation Process*. Mouton, 1971.

Ramanujan, A. K. "On Translating a Tamil Poem." *The Art of Translation: Voices from the Field*, edited by Rosanna Warren, Northeastern UP, 1989, pp. 47–63.

Sakai, Naoki. "Translation and the Figure of Border: Toward the Apprehension of Translation as a Social Action." *Profession*, 2010, pp. 25–34.

—. *Translation and Subjectivity: On "Japan" and Cultural Nationalism*. U of Minnesota P, 1997.

Schleiermacher, Friedrich. "On the Different Methods of Translating." Translated by Susan Bernofsky. *The Translation Studies Reader*, edited by Lawrence Venuti, Routledge, 2012, pp. 43–63.

Schopenhauer, Arthur. "On Language and Words." Translated by Peter Mollenhauer. *Theories of Translation: An Anthology of Essays from Dryden to Derrida*, edited by Rainer Schulte and John Biguenet, U of Chicago P, 1992, pp. 32–35.

Schulte, Rainer and John Biguenet, editors. *Theories of Translation: An Anthology of Essays from Dryden to Derrida*. U of Chicago P, 1992.

Schwerner, Armand. *The Tablets*. Orono: National Poetry Foundation, 1999.

Scott, Clive. *Translating Baudelaire*. U of Exeter P, 2000.

Spivak, Gayatri. "The Politics of Translation." *Outside in the Teaching Machine*. Routledge, 1993, pp. 200–25.

Steiner, George. *After Babel: Aspects of Language and Translation*. Oxford UP, 1998.

—. "Marrow versus marrow." *Times Literary Supplement*, 3 Aug. 2012.

Strand, Mark. *The Continuous Life*. Alfred A. Knopf, 1990.

Šalamun, Tomaž. *The Four Questions of Melancholy: New and Selected Poems*, edited by Christopher Merrill, White Pine P, 1997.

—. *Woods and Chalices*. Translated by Brian Henry and Tomaž Šalamun, Harcourt, 2008.

Šteger, Aleš. *The Book of Things*. Translated by Brian Henry, BOA Editions, 2010.

Tiffany, Daniel. *Radio Corpse: Imagism and the Cryptaesthetic of Ezra Pound*. Harvard UP, 1995.

Trakl, Georg. *Song of the Departed: Selected Poems of Georg Trakl*. Translated by Robert Firmage, Copper Canyon P, 2012.

Valéry, Paul. "Variations on the *Eclogues*." Translated by Denise Folliot. *Theories of Translation: An Anthology of Essays from Dryden to Derrida*, edited by Rainer Schulte and John Biguenet, U of Chicago P, 1992.

Venuti, Lawrence. *The Translator's Invisibility*. Routledge, 1995.

—. ed. *The Translation Studies Reader*. Routledge, 2012.

Waldrop, Rosmarie. *Dissonance (if you are interested)*. U of Alabama P, 2005.

Weinberger, Eliot. "Anonymous Sources." *Oranges and Peanuts for Sale*. New Directions, 2009, pp. 170–84.

—. *Works on Paper*. New Directions, 1986.

About the Author

Brian Henry is the author of twelve books of poetry, most recently *Permanent State* (Threadsuns, 2020). He co-edited the international magazine *Verse* from 1995 to 2018 and established the Tomaž Šalamun Prize in 2015. He has translated Tomaž Šalamun's *Woods and Chalices* (Harcourt, 2008), Aleš Debeljak's *Smugglers* (BOA, 2015), and five books by Aleš Šteger. His translation of Šteger's *The Book of Things* (BOA Editions, 2010) won the Best Translated Book Award and the Best Literary Translation into English Award. His poetry and translations have received numerous honors, including two NEA fellowships, a Howard Foundation grant, the Cecil B. Hemley Memorial Award, the Alice Fay di Castagnola Award, the George Bogin Memorial Award, and a Slovenian Academy of Arts and Sciences grant. He lives in Richmond, Virginia.

Photograph of the author by Tara Rebele. Used by permission.

www.ingramcontent.com/pod-product-compliance
Ingram Content Group UK Ltd.
Pitfield, Milton Keynes, MK11 3LW, UK
UKHW042014190726
13854UKWH00005B/2278

9 781643 172903